FASHION COLORING BOOK FOR TEENAGE GIRLS

Copyright © 2020 Katrin Stark

ALL RIGHTS RESERVED

This Book Belongs To:

COLOR TEST PAGE

More coloring books from Katrin Stark

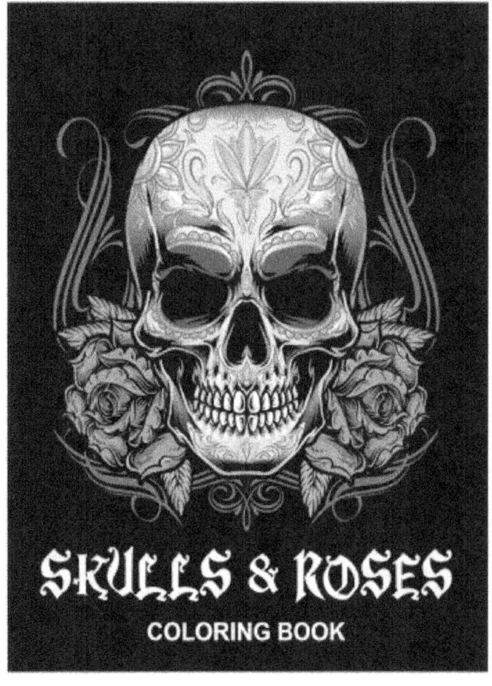

Thank you for buying this book

If you like the book, please consider leaving a review,

it will help author to create better books in the future

www.amazon.com/Katrin-Stark
www.amazon.co.uk/Katrin-Stark